Sneaker Marauders

Names, characters, places and incidents are products of the authors' imaginations or have been used fictitiously and are not to be construed as real. Any resemblance to persons, living or dead, actual events, locales or organizations is entirely coincidental.

ISBN: 978-1-961753-14-3 (Paperback)
ISBN: 978-1-961753-15-0 (Ebook)

First Edition

10 9 8 7 6 5 4 3 2

Black and Square,
an imprint of 45 Alternate Press, LLC
Hampton, Virginia

Sneaker Marauders

Poems

Ran Walker

Van G. Garrett

Black
and
Square

Praise for Sneaker Marauders

Van Garrett and Ran Walker form a perfect poetic team-up, just like my 1985 white/white Adidas Superstar shell toes with white/grey checkerboard fat laces.

Unlike those kicks, a product of its time that we speak of in proud past-tense, like 'well, you had to be there' . . . be joyful, because Garrett and Walker are *here*. *Now*.

Sneaker Marauders will forever be carbonated for freshness - from now to infinity. And guess what? Your size is in stock and I called ahead — they're leaving this for you at the register.

— Jamar Nicholas, author/illustrator
of *LEON the Extraordinary*

Contents

Part One
I Left My Sneakers in El Segundo
25-Word Introduction 3

1. I. 5
2. II. 6
3. III 7
4. IV 8
5. V 9
6. VI 10
7. VII 11
8. VIII 12
9. IX 13
10. X 14
11. XI 15
12. XII 16
13. XIII 17
14. XIV 18
15. XV 19
16. XVI 20
17. XVII 21
18. XVIII 22
19. XIX 23
20. XX 24
21. XXI 25
22. XXII 26
23. XXIII 27
24. XXIV 28
25. XXV 29
26. XXVI 30
27. XXVII 31
28. XXVIII 32

29. XXIX   33
30. XXX   34
31. XXXI   35
32. XXXII   36
33. XXXIII   37
34. XXXIV   38
35. XXXV   39
36. XXXVI   40
37. XXXVII   41
38. XXXVIII   42
39. XXXIX   43
40. XL   44
41. XLI   45
42. XLII   46
43. XLIII   47
44. XLIV   48
45. XLV   49
46. XLVI   50
47. XLVII   51
48. XLVIII   52
49. XLIX   53
50. L   54
51. LI   55

Part Two
Scenarios

Introduction   59
52. For the Love of the Air Max 1, Part 1   61
53. Superman Wore Air Force 1s   62
54. The "It" Girls   63
55. Patta   64
56. Black Cement 3   65
57. SNKRS Saturdays   66
58. Gel-Lyfe   67
59. Ferocious   68

60. GS — 69

61. Come On, Travis — 70

62. Ahab — 71

63. Jokes and Truths — 72

64. Tales from the Old School — 73

65. Sacai Waffles — 74

66. A Ma Maniére — 75

67. Zebras Are Not Pandas — 76

68. The Debate — 77

69. Call It Sweet Nothings If You Want — 78

70. Atmos, the Cartographer — 79

71. Silhouette Devotee — 80

72. For the Love of the Air Max 1, Part 2 — 81

73. Sole Tasting — 82

74. Creps — 83

75. East Side Golf — 84

76. One Day I'll Grow Trees — 85

77. Generation Z — 86

78. Young Love — 87

79. My Grails Are Everywhere — 88

80. Jae Tips — 89

81. Sneaker Freaker — 90

82. Whitner's Masterclass — 91

83. Pandemic Superpowers — 92

84. August — 93

85. The Quest Continues — 94

86. Spike Lee — 95

87. Just One — 96

88. The Collecting Gene — 97

89. Joe Freshgoods — 98

90. King Richard III — 99

91. Should I Buy a Clown Nose Now or
Later? — 100

92. What Anthony Edwards Dreams
About — 101

93. Matriculation ... 102
94. Forgotten Grail ... 103
95. Clash of the Brothers ... 104
96. Unc and The 12s ... 105
97. Black AF ... 106
98. Hiroshi Fujiwara ... 107
99. The First Step ... 108
100. Bobbito the Great ... 109
101. How Do I Say Goodbye? ... 110
102. For the Love of the Air Max 1, Part 3 ... 111

Acknowledgments ... 113
About the Authors ... 115
Also by Ran Walker ... 117
Also by Van G. Garrett ... 119

In Memory of DJ Clark Kent and Phife Dawg

"Sneakers speak louder than words."

— Unknown

Part One

I Left My Sneakers in El Segundo

A Micro Saga-In-Verse

25-Word Introduction

I owe so much to Hip-Hop

Groups like **Tribe** helped me
To find my path as an artist
Poet
Independent thinker
Musician
Man

I'm grateful

- Van G. Garrett

I.

Have you ever experienced
A shoe desert
Inside your closet

Where shoes are
Dry as tumbleweeds
And flat like the paddles
Of dead prickly pears

II.

I've been there—
In the desert—
Rattlesnakes nipping
At my heels
Taunting me to get new kicks
To kick up things
Like a dust storm

III

That's how I ended up
Touring El Segundo…
On a quest
Chasing
Without a tribe
Instinctively
Searching for the perfect pair
Like the perfect beat

IV

I hopped into my jeep
Turned up the music
And headed south
With barely enough money
For gas
Enchiladas

Fruit punch

Feeling lucky as Lucien

V

It's interesting
What people
Will do
To find
What
They think
Will make them happy

I'm the last to judge

I drove days for sneakers

VI

I was like Don Quixote
And TLC—
Chasing windmills
And waterfalls

Without a map
Or plan
Just a hunch
Vibe
Sensation
Deep in my gut

VII

I had ideas
For days
About life in the desert

Stale air and grit
On my face

Covering me like a blanket

Except my shoes

VIII

Man—
Those shoes were fire:
White
Clean as a *Q-Tip*
Without blemish
Or consequence

Shaheed!

From the top
To the low end

*A *Chef's* kiss

*Jarobi

IX

The road waved
Warped
And bumped at
Visions—
Like a mirage

I had driven for hours
Scooping peanut butter
With my finger
From a jar

X

Hunger struck a chord
I had to get food
Pulled into a fast food
Station
Ordered five fish tacos
That made me bubble
Like sewer

XI

The waitress made
Small talk
Knew I wasn't from there:

Here on business

Or love

Eyeing me
And my naked
Ring finger

I smiled—

Both

XII

I drowned chips
Into fire-red salsa
That swam in a worn bowl
Shaped like a sombrero

The color of mustard

Chipped deep
In the ceramic

XIII

She was *bonita*
With an apple bum

I could've put her on

But hot sneakers
Were on my platter

The chit-chit-chatter
Would have to wait

XIV

I got back on the road
That stretched
Like a yawn
An imagination
A space program
A youthful expression—

The lengthy description
Of a fool

XV

I thought about
Tigers
Elephants
And bears

Hummed the soundtrack
Of the circus
The one more popular than
Air Jordan Ones
(Mid):

Entry of the Gladiators

XVI

It's random
I know
But it reminds me of a song
That I like
By **A Tribe Called Quest**
About Kamaal Fareed
Misplacing his wallet

XVII

There's a long stretch
Of Earth
From Texas to California

Twists and turns
Like jazz

Abstract thoughts:
Remixed scenarios

Eight million stories
That boom bap

XVIII

My mind was a lawnmower
Shredding thoughts and
Making room
For new ideas
To sprout

I thought about my favorite
Sneakers
Colorways
And hard-earned grails

XIX

Lows
Dunks
Maxes
Classics
Vintage
Exclusives
Those worn while
Doing chores
Or stepping out
Or driving
Across the country—
Keeping things rolling
On a humbug

XX

I arrived—
Two days later—
Before midnight—
Like a marauder—

On the beach

The spot that Fred Sanford quipped
And ATCQ echoed

AKA: *The Second*

XXI

I wanted to kiss
The boardwalk
Like Malcolm pressed
Mecca

The place
Where dreams glowed
Like gems:

A symbol of hope

Like *The Black Stone*

XXII

I washed under the spigot
Of a public shower
Sand a silent audience
As water flowed through grates
As I beatboxed
And daydreamed about sneakers

XXIII

Feet up
Facing a fire pit
Taking in the moment
Flashbacks
And flickers of memories

I wanted roasted corn
Ceviche
Street tacos
Watermelon
And more

XXIV

I pulled a peanut butter
And jelly sandwich
From my pack
Like a rabbit
From a hat

Closed my eyes

And listened to the surf

XXV

I woke
Focused
Saw two figures
Near a volleyball net

A woman and her dog
Silhouetted
Against orange
Like a postcard

I had to speak…

XXVI

I try to choose
My words
Wisely

Like a poet

Carefully

Without overusing
Superlatives
For everything that causes
Me to pause

Reflect

Notice

And think…

XXVII

I rarely use words
Like:
Legend
Icon
Hero
Genius
Or muse
But when I do
The words
Hit

She was a
Muse

Yes—
A
Muse

XXVIII

She was fire
Like a dungeon dragon

I didn't want her
As a concubine

I had to know her

Before taking her

To St. Elsewhere

XXIX

Beautiful smile
Thick as cheese grits
Hips and curves
That would make you
Want to clap your hands

But I didn't

I'm not a sucker…

XXX

I treaded lightly
In the sand

Didn't do too much
Stayed calm

Wanted to know her name
And figure out how
She outshined the sun

XXXI

Her butter-smooth skin
Glowed
Magically
Like ice
Against my hockey puck
Complexion
When I shook her hand

I'm Van

I'm Benita

Nice to meet you…

XXXII

Benita
Benita
Benita

Her name hummed
Like the chorus
Of a familiar song

She was fine

A top priority

She had to put me on…

XXXIII

Her voice was like choirs
And church bells
Ringing
At Christmas

A Trini from the UK
Almond-shaped eyes
Glistening like diamonds
And glinting like stars

XXXIV

She likes you

I looked down

Extended the meaty part

Of my hand

To a Teacup Yorkie

That lapped my skin

Like a savory roti

XXXV

It was like every word
Had handles
The way that I held on
To her every lip curl

There was something REALLY
    special
About her…

XXXVI

You came all this way
For sneakers

I thought about what she asked

How she said it—

Without judgement

Looked at her
Intently:

Not sure…

XXXVII

Everything was cinematic
No exaggeration
Slow panning
Vignettes
As we talked
Until the orange sun
Turned into a cherry moon
That we belly laughed under

XXXVIII

We talked about things
That rhyme with Luke Cage
Loot cakes
Sticks
Kicks
Prophylactics
Determined
Loving
Excursions
Trips
Q-Tip
Mali
Ali
Macaroni
Jarobi
Life
Phife

XXXIX

My stomach out-growled a bear

I elbowed myself

The way one does

Embarrassed

By a misplaced joke

She didn't laugh

Or skip a single beat

XL

Let's grab breakfast

I'll drive

I didn't know how
I would fit
Inside her Fiat 500

Knees to the dash

Dog cradled in my lap

XLI

I couldn't feel
My legs
As we drove to the restaurant

It had nothing
Yet everything
To do with the
Tight space
That we shared

XLII

Conversations bubbled
Like soap
At The Kettle
Over panko chicken tenders—
California fries—
Loaded with scallions and
Avocado buttermilk ranch
That flowed
Like the ocean

XLIII

Breakfast was *non-traditional*
But we went with it
And enjoyed
Taking turns
Sneaking some chicken
To Tokyo
Happy as a clam
Tail-wagging
In the car

XLIV

But all good things
Must come to an end
Or pause
She had to get to work
I had to get my jeep
And jet

XLV

We didn't part ways
Abruptly
Without tying up
A loose end:

You're not leaving
Without getting
What you came here for

Confusion landscaped my face...

XLVI

You drove all this way
For kicks

I got you

Do you rock Vans

She took out her phone
Asked my size
Sent a text

XLVII

When we pulled up at the beach
Her cousin was waiting—
Like Santa Clause—
Two shoe boxes in hand

He nodded

Handed her the shoes

XLVIII

Hope you like these—
They're not rare…

She handed me the box
In my size

A pair of traditional
Black and white checkerboard
Vans slip-on's

XLIX

I was speechless
As tides inside me
Rushed like the waves

I hugged her
Like a lover

Her cousin
Stared blankly
At the rising sun

L

She got the same pair

We're SOLEMATES

She took an eyeliner pencil
From her fanny pack
Autographed
The inside of my shoes

Now they're exclusives

LI

I hated to leave
The place
That appeared
As unexpectedly
As a marauder

But I loved
How daydreams
Of sneakers
Turned my hopes
Into realities

Part Two

Scenarios

Prose Poems

Introduction

And Tinker stepped out on space, and he looked around and said, "This is boring. It's time to change the game."

For the Love of the Air Max 1, Part I

Amsterdam heat. Too hot for most American streets. We don't run no more, just walk the beat, air beneath our feet. These kicks so dope I collab with myself, high-five Tinker, fresher than Pringles with the seal just popped, like Grandma just slapped the taste out of my mouth.

Superman Wore Air Force 1s

For DJ Clark Kent

Superman wore Air Force 1s when he was incognegro in the studio or behind the turntables, heads nodding to the beat, heads nodding to the feet. But this hero was more Gotham than Krypton, more Kesha than Lois, more OG than labels that brands use for marketing. Superman was a real one, a legend, if ever there was one, and the hole he left in the Culture will never be filled, only respected, a crater where he landed and changed the world around him.

The "It" Girls

The girls stand in a semi-circle popping chewing gum, their sneakers an array of colors like Gobstoppers, whispering to each other about who is cute and whose kicks are the dopest—and how it seems nearly impossible to find someone with both.

Patta

Not onomatopoeia, but Surinamese Creole,
Blackness in Amsterdam crushing images of
Zwarte Piet beneath waffle outsoles and air cush-
ions, fists raised proudly for the diaspora to see
and know that, yes, we are here—in full effect.

Black Cement 3

"I have the original '88 pair in my collection," the teacher remarked, nodding at the sneakers of one of his students.

He wasn't trying to become a Jedi master that day, but to his class, that is exactly what he became.

SNKRS Saturdays

Saturday morning endorphins higher than giraffe nuts, phone clutched in my hand like I'm holding it over the Grand Canyon, I am beyond ready. Watching the seconds tick by until 10 AM EST strikes, then seeing how fast my fingers can move, as if SNKRS is not a lottery and "first come/first served" is still the law of the land.

Gel-Lyfe

No tongue, but my Gel-Lyte IIIs are talking much
trash today, Feig and Atmos co-signing like the
loan's come due. I'm fresh to death, and, yeah, it's
one of those "if you know" thangs.

Ferocious

These kicks are ferocious, like Doechii petting an alligator or Minnie Riperton petting a lion or a tamer taming the untamable, these kicks marching through the jungle, taking no prisoners, burning the ship, prepared to conquer all that lies before them.

GS

She sees them watching, faces full of envy, but she can't help that she can get away with paying less. Sometimes there *are* perks to having smaller feet.

Come On, Travis

I know it was likely a publicity stunt, but McEnroe had it right: the sneaker should have been called the Cactus Mac.

Ahab

For Bobbito

The Moby Dick of Sneakerheads lives somewhere on this side of town, I am convinced. The local Goodwill has become the top spot to cop for the most coveted kicks, heads lined up around the corner to cop a size 11M in whatever they have in stock this week.

He's out there somewhere, lurking, hooking the rest of us up, keeping the sport of searching alive and well for the next generation.

Jokes and Truths

On *Family Guy*, Cleveland jokes about buying his Yeezys on clearance, and somewhere, off in the distance, a tear falls from the eye of a reseller.

Tales from the Old School

Uncle Jamar regales the kids with stories of walking into the basements of mom & pops, combing through their old sneakers and making out like a bandit.

"Nowadays," he says through exasperation, "you can just go to a reseller website and buy them. Where's the fun in that?"

They look at him, shaking their heads, forgiving him for being old school, though secretly wishing they had been there, too.

Sacai Waffles

The combined midsoles made him feel as though he could leap at the moon and touch it. He was a dreamer, and it was important for a dreamer's feet to never touch the ground.

A Ma Maniére

Maroon and mauve, burgundy and black,
redefining the colors of the rainbow in Blackness,
my feet are wrapped in its luxury, its name the
only French to roll off my tongue since the 8th
grade.

Zebras Are Not Pandas

He had heard somewhere a zebra's stripes helped to confuse predators who, when they saw zebras standing in groups, couldn't distinguish their individual forms.

He later read that was not true and that stripes did not, in fact, represent any kind of camouflage.

Still, it didn't stop him from thinking about that as he stared at a group of teens wearing Panda Dunks at the mall.

The Debate

Even more intense than the debate about the Oxford comma is the debate about whether or not sail laces go with every sneaker.

Call It Sweet Nothings If You Want

After good loving, she whispers sweet colorways into his ear while he takes a hit and passes it back to her, his smile as wide as a Cheshire cat's.

Atmos, the Cartographer

He can see his neighborhood in the grid of the NYC subway lines, and he gives Asics the nod for getting those Gel-Lyte IIIs right.

Silhouette Devotee

His boys cracked on him because he only wore one silhouette and had every other colorway in a collection that took up three walls. His social media handles were devoted to the model, and even the brand reached out to him to have him spit some knowledge on the silhouette for a documentary.

Once, he was gifted a pair of kicks that were not only a different model, but a different brand. The debate still rages as to whether or not he donated them immediately afterwards or flipped them online.

For the Love of the Air Max 1, Part 2

She dreams of Tinker standing outside the Pompidou, gathering inspiration for the ultimate sneaker, wondering what the sneaker game might be like if he hadn't visited Paris that fateful day.

Sole Tasting

My little cousin asked me, apropos of nothing, "Why these ninjas out here licking soles?"

It was such a profound question, one for which I had no answer.

Creps

He loved creps with crepe soles, loved to sit cross-legged outside a café eating crêpes, glancing down at his shoes and thinking to himself, "Does life get any better than this?"

East Side Golf

He yells, "The House!" instead of "Fore!" because you never stop repping for the brothers at 830 Westview Dr., SW; Atlanta, GA 30314.

One Day I'll Grow Trees

One day she will sell her entire collection and buy a pair of biodegradable sneakers she can just plant into the ground once she's worn them down. In the meantime, she is fixated on putting at least five miles on each of the shoes she owns to justify having owned them.

Generation Z

He never saw Jordan play, but you wouldn't know it from his collection.

Young Love

They had considered getting matching tattoos, but getting matching kicks made more sense.

My Grails Are Everywhere

Those sneakers are balloons sailing into the heavens until Nike walks into the room and retros them, bringing them back down to Earth.

Jae Tips

Summertime is here! Baseball caps, beards, and flowers! We knee-deep in cotton, pinks, and violets, dancing in the bend of the Sacony Creek, feet feeling fresh in mesh, smiles on our faces. We not like them, and they not like us, and that's all right.

Sneaker Freaker

Down Under, old heads whip out trainers from the days of Voltron, catching aficionados looking, fingering twenties in their wallets, wanting to cop what they see, but in Melbourne they don't do twinsies. Originality is the only currency that matters.

Whitner's Masterclass

Neville didn't know anything about cracked leather, crushed velvet, or quilted insoles, but he could sense these shoes were more luxurious than others in his collection and that he was now becoming more of a sneaker aficionado than merely a sneakerhead.

Pandemic Superpowers

The talent he picked up during the pandemic was how to clean sneakers. Hours of YouTube videos, hours of cultivating the best cleaners, hours of practicing an array of techniques made him a force of nature. When he returned to campus in the fall, he set up shop next to the dorm barber and set out to pay off his student loans.

August

With the moon as full as a tick, she straddled him on one of the swings down the street from her apartment building, her Air Max 90s kicking one direction, his Air Max 95s kicking the other. The summer had finally come to an end, and their "situationship" hung delicately in the balance between nostalgia and curiosity of the unknown, their bodies oscillating back and forth between the two.

The Quest Continues

His grandmother made the mistake of asking him which sneakers he wanted for his birthday. She gave him $500 to work with. In some respects, this should have been a no-brainer for him, but he found himself deliberating heavily, Chat GPT-ing his options relentlessly, as if this would be the only chance he would have, in life, to score a grail. His wishlist was long, and it never crossed his mind to get multiple pairs, only to go after the biggest of the fish.

Three weeks after his birthday, he was still undecided, combing sneaker sites and mall resell stores, fixated on finding the perfect pair.

In the end, he took the cash and, as of the writing of this story, has still not selected a pair of sneakers.

Spike Lee

Not that I have seen every sneaker that Spike has worn in public, but I can't remember ever seeing him wear a pair of Spizikes, highs or lows, at least in recent memory. He's had hella heat out and about, but never really rocked his own shoe.

If I had my own shoe, would I wear it all the time in different colorways? I would think so. After all, it *is* my shoe. But when you have access to so much heat, is it reasonable to think you would rock one silhouette publicly for the rest of your days? I guess Spike knows that answer already.

Just One

Remember what it was like to have just one pair, like Miles Morales? Just rocking the same joints day in and day out, and everyone knew that was your shoe, and you kind of owned it, like you were an official endorser of the brand. And because you had that one pair, you had to baby it like one might a new leather glove before the beginning of the baseball season. And in the end, they would be dogged, despite constant cleaning and ironing and whatever else you did to preserve their freshness. Then you'd get another pair and start the cycle again.

Man, I miss those days.

The Collecting Gene

How do you know when you have too many sneakers? The statement sounds like the setup for a dad joke, but in reality it is the philosophical dilemma many sneakerheads confront. Is there a specific number, or is it about volume and how much space they take up? You have two feet and 100 pairs of sneakers. The logic is not there, yet it kind of is. Maybe it's the same thing as asking can you have too many baseball cards or Hot Wheels cars or playing card decks or stamps or books. Is there an unequivocal answer to such a question?

My brother once said it was not hoarding if you cared and cultivated the things you collected.

Joe Freshgoods

He writes a poem about Joe Freshgood's New Balance 900 v3 "Outside Clothes," but when he goes to write a line in the past participle form about cutting the grass, he gets stuck on "mowed" versus "mown," the latter sounding better for a poem, the former sounding practical for conversation. He must now ask himself who is this poem for. For himself? Then is he a "mowed" person or a "mown" person, and, even more interestingly, what kind of grass was Joe Freshgoods thinking about when he designed the shoe?

King Richard III

My cousin Tre often says, "My kingdom for a pair of Js!"

Sometimes I wonder if he gets the reference, or if he's just talking.

Should I Buy a Clown Nose
Now or Later?

He wants to pull the trigger on the Lost and Found Jordan 1s, but he is afraid of how they will look on his size 15 feet.

What Anthony Edwards
Dreams About

The dream: to be in a commercial, drinking a Sprite while dunking on some hapless kid in a way that showcases the AE 1 (or 2), only to come out of the commercial and dunk on some joker in real life during Game 7 of the NBA finals in the last three seconds of the fourth quarter to seal the deal for the Timberwolves and garner the finals MVP.

Matriculation

Last year, it was Jordans and Yeezys. This year it's New Balances and Asics. Next year it will be something different, these kids. But whatever it is, I'm here for it.

Forgotten Grail
For A Tribe Called Quest

The AJ1 "A Tribe Called Quest," splashed in ragged red, black, and green stripes, like their album covers, though coveted by many heads they are not, but then collecting doesn't always make sense, when flipping gets in the way of wearing, and that damn collar strap gives ninjas fits. Still, I rock with them, always have, always will, like a DOOM Dunk or a culinary masterpiece by Jarobi.

Clash of the Brothers

I tried to tell this dude he couldn't wear Puma and Adidas together. *It's a civil war of the fit*, I said.

The Dassler brothers hated each other so much they're buried at opposite ends of the same cemetery. To this day, people in Herzogenaurach don't deal with each other over this, so, no, young brother, your arbitrary mismatching does not make you an arbiter for this feud. Go somewhere and sit down and learn some history.

Unc and The 12s

My uncle liked to flex his Jordan 12s on the block.

"Them young'uns don't know about these!"

Dookie gold rope. Coogi sweater. Jeans pressed. Shoes cleaner than the board of health.

"You can bury me in these," he once told me.

We did.

Black AF

I'm Blacker than a hundred midnights down in a cypress swamp*, like some beat black Air Force 1s on a K. Dot cover, like Jordan black cats, like Patta fists, like the Black history collab every brand wants to get right, like shell toes with no laces, like the smell of cocoa butter behind scorched ears, like finding love at the block party, like Frankie Beverly and cookouts, like the souls of the White Lion.

---

* From "The Creation" by James Weldon Johnson

Hiroshi Fujiwara

Quiet beauty, whispers across fabric and leather, the lightning bolts move in tandem like two dobermans whose silky black coats demand respect without them ever having bared their fangs.

The First Step

One day he walked into his room and was overcome by the thick smell of rubber, leather, and mesh. It was only then that he realized he had a sneaker problem.

Bobbito the Great

Cucumber slices are good for the souls/soles, whether on project playgrounds, streetball courts, studios, or the crackling vinyl grooves of DOOM. Legendary is a way of life, like the hunt, the exploration of greatness, and heads want to ask where I got those gems, well, they should already know.

How Do I Say Goodbye?

He remembers the day he saw them at the mall, how lucky he felt they had them in his size, how his boys had asked about them and the girls thought he was fly, how it felt to see their value go up on the secondary market, how he knew he would never sell them, and how painful it was to see the soles crumble like cookies, dust and airbags, faded dye of the leather.

He must now ask if he wants to do a sole swap and get them repaired or let them go on to that great sneaker store in the sky. If only there was insurance for this moment. He knows it is more financially prudent to let them go, but the thought of having another go-round with them for a few more years proves too tantalizing to pass up.

For the Love of the Air Max 1, Part 3

He loves it when she rocks her Air Max 1s, her sculpted legs shining with shea butter, beautiful brown like mochas, her smile the helium that makes him float on air.

Acknowledgments

Ran Walker would like to thank his wife and daughter for putting up with him and his sneaker addiction (which he is slowly taming) and cheering him on as he wrote this book.

Van G. Garrett would like to thank the Betsy Hotel for awarding him a Writer's Room Fellowship. The dedicated time and space to work on this book was invaluable.

About the Authors

Ran Walker (he/him) is an award-winning writer, filmmaker, musician, and creative writing professor. He lives with his wife and daughter in Virginia. Feel free to check him out at ranwalker.com.

Van G. Garrett (he/him) is a sneakerhead, musician, visual artist, creative writing instructor, and the author of the picture book *Kicks*. Check out Van's updates at www.vanggarrettpoet.com.

Also by Ran Walker

B-Sides and Remixes

30 Love: A Novel

Mojo's Guitar: A Novel / (Il était une fois Morris Jones)

Afro Nerd in Love: A Novella

The Keys of My Soul: A Novel

The Race of Races: A Novel

The Illest: A Novella

Bessie, Bop, or Bach: Collected Stories

Four Floors (with Sabin Prentis)

Black Hand Side: Stories

White Pages: A Novel

She Lives in My Lap

Reverb

Work-In-Progress

Daykeeper

Most of My Heroes Don't Appear On No Stamps

Portable Black Magic: Tales of the Afro Strange

The Strange Museum: 50-Word Stories

Bees + Things + Flowers: Microfictions

The World Is Yours: Microfictions

Can I Kick It?: Sneaker Microfiction and Poetry (with Van G. Garrett)

The Golden Book: A 50-Year Marriage Told In 50-Word Stories

Keep It 100: 100-Word Stories

A Burst of Gray: A Novel In 100-Word Stories

The Library of Afro Curiosities: 100-Word Stories

Black Marker: A Novel in 100-Word Stories

GloKat and the Art of Timing: A Novel in 100-Word Stories

A Different Kind of Christmas Story: A Carol in 100-Word Stories

Spaceships Don't Come Equipped with Rearview Mirrors: 50-Word Stories

This Is Not a Poem/Story: 100-Word Stories

Parts of Speech: 100-Word Stories

Four Suits: A Deck of 100-Word Stories

O'ahu: Prose Poems

Apollo's Toy Box

Gods Among Men

One Hundred Ways: A Handbook for Writing 100-Word Stories

Also by Van G. Garrett

Songs in Blue Negritude

ZURI: Love Songs

The Iron Legs in the Trees

49: Wings & Prayers

Lennox in Twelve: Poems

Hog

Water Bodies: Poems

Pit Bulls and J-Walks

Can I Kick It?: Sneaker Microfiction and Poetry (with Ran Walker)

SCRAP: Kwansabas

Kicks

Juneteenth

A Car Named Emily

Specs

www.ingramcontent.com/pod-product-compliance
Lightning Source LLC
Chambersburg PA
CBHW051212120626
46547CB00013B/1325